The Grace of Falling Things

The Grace of Falling Things

poems

Karl Plank

GRAYSON BOOKS
West Hartford, Connecticut
graysonbooks.com

For my mother, Joyce Clayton Plank
and
In memory of my father, Charles Andrews Plank

Contents

Rain and the Ground It Falls Upon

Gravity

Witnessed in the First Month of the Year

To this I swear:

One winter afternoon, late,
as the sky softened in subtlety,
a mated pair of red-tails
circled in a *pas de deux* of magic light,
curling down to the broken elbow
of the bare winged elm,
their hollow bones landing
in utter synchrony.

No hoarse hissy screech
downslurred to tear the air
and when talons gripped the branch
no vibration disturbed the tracery
of long, black fingers, skeletal streaks
of calligraphy against a scrim of sky.
No movement, but for the release
of the merest twig at limb's end,
falling tenderly to the earth,
nearly unnoticed.

Gravity

When night calls for sounds
to cease, the barred owl
yet cries "Who cooks for you?"
and somewhere a woman
slippers through the dark
to a kitchen where water drips
a slow beat on the worn basin.
She nooses the tap with string,
a strand that drops to the drain,
and waits for each bead
to catch the thread and
descend into a well of silence
not even night can bring.

For the Time Being

The pin oak at the back corner is listing
though no onrush of wind from the north
pushes it off plumb. It leans on its own,
now still, like the mast of a vessel aground,
bow lifted by the seabed suddenly below.

If we were to walk to the edge of the yard,
past the patch of obedient plants and their spikes
of lavender, we might kneel at the tree base
and offer ear to earth, listening for the strain
of gnarled roots as they grip the underground

to keep in place the leaning trunk, the branches
that reach out from its spine. We might wonder
about the softness of soil after rain and the steady
silence that soothes and holds fast, so different
from the loud crack that blares in our minds

from the rim of tomorrow.

Tools of the Trade

for Cecil V. Clayton, in memoriam

They are here
because they were his.

The carpenter's scribe
with its fence and rail
and the smoothing plane
have no work to do
at this desk where I
labor with words.

They belong to the shop
by the river's side
where he readied the grain
and wrote in wood,
making marks to guide
the precise blade-stroke

that fit the waiting edge.
Next to pens and stray
bull-dog clips, they have
no function but to
revive the memory
of my grandfather's

sturdy hands and how
he spoke with gentle
measure as if to teach
that words gained strength
from the quiet silence
of what had been first

trimmed and cut away.

The Sound of a Tree Falling as We Hear It

The Cat skidder wards us off our usual path
past the rangy pines and the tallgrass
to the Chinese hawthorn with its berries of red sun.

We are forbidden by the caution color of mustard metal
and grist-bite of gears. Two men walk through mud,
chain saws 4-stroking, fingers curled at the trigger.

We know what we will hear next: the hum racing, brattling,
blade teeth engaging, the noise that blasts before the crack
of long-leaf pine giving way at its base   and the silence

as it topples through the air. We have turned back to see,
as if the interrupting silence had called us by name
to witness the downfall.

It takes more time than one imagines, this downfall.
The felled tree does not plummet,
but slips through atmosphere

that gentles the descent
of what it cannot hold aloft.
This the grace of falling things.

Tarblooder

on this altar a railroad spike
rests its offset head
a relic of iron bone and skeleton

and we should care i tell you
because the secret of prayer
is the sound of the tarblooder

driving steel into the wooden sleeper
on the track bed
each blow of the hammer

a violent gravity sending hot tar
upward to splatter on bared arms
until blood drips on crossties

nailed to the earth

Doxology

from whom all blessings flow
like warmed blood
falling through rubber tubes
to find channels in rivulets
of the veins, of the vanity
of *creatures here below*
who did not hear ice calve
in the faraway and think of hearts
breaking apart and the seep of sorrow
that leaves bodies cold, in need
of this dripping grace even to whisper
Praise God.

Descent in Blue

after Georgia O'Keeffe's "Abstraction Blue" (1927)

A body plunging in arctic water
wants to protect itself
with arms encircling
to shield the head from shattering.
Yet already a crack widens
from the spear-tip of descent.
Damage wrecks symmetry.
One halved skull edges ahead
in a race to the depths,
the momentum of fracture, we think,
unless it is the body's own jagged repair,
arms closing to press in place
bits of bone that will not again align.

At the Edge of the Pond

after Georgia O'Keeffe, "Pond in the Woods" (1922)

We look into the pond as if peering down a well,
eyes descending on glazed spiral-rims of green,
blue, and brown that narrow coil by coil
in a dizzy path to the bottom.
There waits a slice of moon,
an off-centered smile edged in yellow.
It tempts, this, the waning remains of skylight,
a broken bit of cookie sinking past curling lips
of the whorl that finally has no bottom
as it has no surface.
There is only the falling and depths
where green drips into nothing we can see.

Sky Above Clouds

after Joanne Wong's photograph, "Sky Above Clouds IV"
(Georgia O'Keeffe's "Sky Above Clouds IV" at the Art Institute
of Chicago)

I see you descending stairs
approaching the landing,
raven-haired, black-suited,
your shoulder bag, a white wing tucked tight,
left hand only grazing the rail.
To the left and right, other flights of stairs
taking you down.
But before you, a choice
of art's possibility,
the vast opening of skyscape,
the frame, a threshold
that is yours to step through
and leave behind for the beyond,
an endless floor of white floes
grouted with undercurrents of azure,
these your steppingstones to the far, fair lines
of horizons untouched,
known only to those who soar,
believing they will not fall.

Precarity

after Georgia O'Keeffe, "From a Day at Esther's" (1976-1977)

This moment will not last.
A blue circle sits on a tabletop
of identical color,
a flat horizontal bar
like two others
more intensely blue
stacked beneath it,
firm, level ground,
we might think,
for the world to rest upon.
And those crossbeams,
what do they rest upon,
someone asks.
This is not the Hindu tale
of one elephant standing
on top of another
all the way down,
for this last mesa
balances on the round edge
of one more circle.
Already weight is shifting,
pieces chipping off,
the first downfall
before Pedernal topples
into the yellow fluff
of cottonwood trees,
leaving the sun
to drop on crumbling horizons.
But isn't it beautiful,
we must add,
Piedra Lumbre, shining stone
mountain, lake, and star,

this instant of poise,
the grace of line and curve
on the eve of whatever comes after.

A Ladder in the Sky

after Georgia O'Keeffe, "Ladder to the Moon" (1958)

Once a ladder rested its feet firmly in the clay
and its side rails reached the night sky.
Angels scampered up and down the rungs
like children at recess.
The earth as playground, you might have observed,
recalling the dreamscape before waking to alarms,
day's exposure of desert.
The angels have gone away,
the ladder adrift in turquoise like a tailless kite
whose string escaped your grasp,
giving itself to whims of wind
and whirs of unseen wings.
Only the rocky bed of Pedernal remains,
gravity's child,
and the crescent nick on the sky's scrim,
a way out, you think.

The Beyond

after Georgia O'Keeffe, "The Beyond" (1972)

The beyond has a ledge washed in white paint
that we might stand upon,
a balance beam across the horizon
and yet above it as if suspended,
unsupported in blue air.
It is the rim of the next horizon,
this second line of sky's fringe,
that draws us to jump into nothingness,
onto the transom of the farther side of vision.
Our toes curl at the edge,
necks craned to see something still more as, near-blind,
you must have done in this final painting.
The desert avails, opens at last to seas of color,
wavings of the beyond,
and now here you are, leaping into it.

Nightfall

Guardian of Our Breath

Doorman, keeper of the entry-way
and passage for parting, give her
the red-seeded wand as your pledge.
Guard this limen from noxious
spirits, from stridor and the barking
cough. Watch as she wraps whitethorn
in cinnabar and lays branch and spur
on the lintel of door and hearth
and at windows of rooms where
children sleep. May their breath
flow unmolested. For night comes.

For night has fallen and crossed
the threshold.

Doorman, sentry of beginnings
and *in extremis*, let no mother hear
the wheeze of doom; let no child
gasp for air.

A Window Is a Door

Doorman, a window is a door you can see through,
a break in the wall that lets in light,
lets in the stand of lanky aspen whose petioles quake
to wave gold in this season of the hawkwatch,
lets in the upslurring song of the grosbeak
as it wheets in flight and the reddening eyebrow
of the dusky grouse as it courts its mate,
lets in the fancy of mind as it turns to its own abandon,
anthem, and soaring desire—lets in what is beyond
this place where we stand held by the grille and jamb
that focus our labor, to rub the pane with cloth
until light slips into darkness, the grove recedes,
and our minds, like the birds themselves, grow still,
until, that is, we see in the glass our own face dimly,
peering back at us in the other direction, envisioning
from the shadows all that happened before.

Quiet Night

At year's end, the hermit Paul burned all the baskets
he had made and the hut where he kept them.
Then he began anew to braid strands of palm and prayer
over and under and over again.

Li Bai, it is said, wrote characters that stood like decent gents.
He read his poems to a washerwoman with her stick
before folding them into boats to float downstream.
If he died trying to grab moonlight in the Long River,

he also wrote, *Let us waste not the moon.*

And now, though I know you will not read these words,
I will not squander their moment.
I will write them to spark fire in the desert
and play in the current that bears grief away.

Night Fight

after you have gone you will come to a river and
cross it unaware

i see you at the edge and want to draw you back
but the harness has been cut leather lines and breast-strap
torn loose by strain of muscle and fury so i tug on reins
attached to nothing to strong-arm a glimpse of your eyes
but heave only hollow air and now i can just warn that

on the other side waits Night waits darkness and
the hiding of the moon waits one whose face you
will not see one whose hands bear the silt and effluvium
of the riverbed as they reach out to wrench bone from socket
breath from cage memory from holding cells or to touch and
touch the tender skin as a blessing until you cry the same
words that break the threshold of my own lips
i will not let you go will not let you go not let you go.

Night Prayer

And when you lie down in that place to sleep
the Night will show itself to you
as rods ascending as lights of lapis.

Stone pillows and unlathered ground—
may these give armistice from the war
of waking hours.

We can say it now. There was wreckage.
The history of harm raining on you
coursed through breaks in the skin

and splattered on garments of ivory,
bone and ghost. A house fell to its knees
and you were gone.

Now find the sleeping place that is yours.
Behind shuttered eyes peer into the other
darkness where waits the climbing path

and a voice neither dream nor nightmare.

Easter Vigil

Care, something we ask others to take,
half-believing that caution saves from
risk, the darkness of futures neither you nor
I would enter; we cannot
see what waits in shadow.
This morning we saw the hawk, high and still.
I envied his vision of the minute, the faraway
shiver of the vole, the lack of
regard for all else. Peace nests with
indifference to brown-studied
safety, the need to know we are all right
even though we crawl among the dead,
noticing the splay of arms and legs
and their uneasy tableau.
Lie down and sleep on this pan of clay
level in its welcome to bodies that drop
exhausted. Even fear comes to rest,
leaving darkness on its own
until again there is day,
insistent on its return
and tenacious light.

If This Night God Were You or I

his mind would never romp again like the mind of God
—F. Scott Fitzgerald, *The Great Gatsby*

He says this with regret, as if it were a bad thing,
and we understand how he might long
for such in the short run—to imagine
everything as possible, to behold the world
as fresh as the dew on Eden's grass
and as unspoiled.

We, too, would run barefooted, rollick
and romp in the garden where fruit
hangs low, ripe and ready to pick—
to pick again, I should say, for it feels
as if we have done this before
when we were young.

And therein comes our expectation
that return is in our grasp
as it is in the mind of God,
that we might choose to revisit the scenes
of our innocence and claim endless
opportunities of desire:

the daisy unsnatched from the field;
the plum unplucked, juicy and sweet,
as when we savored it for the first time
and kissed lusciousness with our lips.
We would leap into timelessness,
fly over ground

where we might otherwise live
and frankly should, for the thin air dizzies
in its temptations—such a bounty of blossoms,
such a splay of *les pommes rouges et délicieux*

that await the caress of finger and tongue.
We might get away with it, this divine frolic,

except contemplation is never enough
and our touch returns all to time
where change runs its course and vows
bind. Yet, there is grace in gravity
for where everything is possible,
nothing is.

We fall, but softly—*felix culpa*—
landing not on hardscape stone,
but into the bed of our own making
where awaits the familiar flank
and the brush of hands
at day's end.

Here we know what is ours:
the rumple of warmth, rest in the arms
of another that even God would desire
if He could escape eternity and become,
for just a moment, a human being—
that is, if this night God were you or I.

The Sound of One Poem Tapping

Two prisoners whose cells adjoin communicate with each other by knocking on the wall . . . every separation is a link.
—Simone Weil

these poems are not for you
not for me

but for one left behind
or lost

as when a pilgrim enters a thicket
without end

to cross the world

there are no gates
nor paths of egress for

this one whose breath I hear
ear cupped to the wall

who scratches graffiti
on the other side

with pencil stub and shards
of glass

this one who when night falls
hammers a signal code

rock in hand
that chips away at blocks of stone

to this one I tap out words
in reply

poems   prayers

What the Falling Said

Prayer Before a Sermon in the Nave

Uphold Thou me
that I may lift up
the heavy-hinged hatch
that seals us in the hold
of captive cargo.
We fumble in the dark, hands up
to feel our way in gestures
of surrender or pleadings
to stop, to stay away.
We have touched the walls,
seen the absence of light
and now would ascend
to the trapdoor, a ladder of bodies.
Reach out, I cry, *that I may lift up*
Thee.

Our Sins to Be Confessed

the remembrance of them

is planted in my tongue
like barbwire

comes out of my mouth
like the ripping of soft tissue

bleeds incarnadine
like the stain of seas

made red
like roses and carnations

in funeral wreaths of sorrow
like the regret we feel

when losing what is dear
like the time before days became grave-

bearing weight
like all that *is grievous unto us.*

At the Reading of the Gospel

The Gospel of the caracal
night-roamer
lynx of the desert
beast of the black-tufted ear
wondrous leaper
you who bolt into the air of the wild
to claim your meat
to satisfy a hunger
such as the desperate must feel
before a vow is spoken
that lifts falling eyes
to a book held aloft
a mouth opening
to stammer *of the Lord*.

Thy Kingdom Come

Two rumors have been circulating in town. The one,
how a murder of crows gathered in the corn field while
you played with fiddle and bow. The other
keeps you awake and
involves what happens next, which
no one really knows.
Generally, most suggest the worst,
doling out predictions of ruined harvest,
of stalks stripped bare and ravaged. Their
mouths are mean, but you see where they're
coming from and have wondered the same.
Often it is that way. An excess of
merriment feels like something you should pay
extra for, a judgment requiring forfeit
to balance an unforgiving scale.
How dour this is. And how it makes you
yawn.
When the crows came you saw no cloud of
ill fate, nor saw at all beyond the
luxury of daylight's lifting of
languor, the hot and heavy
burdens hard to escape
except when breezes blow,
daring all to flutter, to dance at least
once in quickening air,
never thinking of how it could end
except in music.

And Also with You

I want for you
what I want myself

breath
the tin-cup of cool water

which I drink and slosh
over my head

hat in one hand
streaked with the salt of sweat

that is the drain
and map of my effort

to move this dirt
from here to there

until I fall upon it
and gasp

the onset of rain my drenching
downpour of peace

Which Passes All Understanding

The peace of God
slices of silence
wafer-thin
dwell in
the interstices
the crevices
and crackle
of fragile lives
as they begin
to shatter.
Stand between
the snap and the howl
that this be not all
we know.
Be not less
on this day
but more
than we can say.

Rain and the Ground It Falls Upon

Four Men, Three Made of Mud

When loss lurches through his mind,
he takes comfort in the miniature—*penjing*.
A landscape of tree and rock entire on its tray.

Thus, he beholds the world without fault,
made as before, but in small scale.
He sits in the company of mudmen

dressed in mustard, cerulean, and celadon.
One figure holds a scroll; another, a moon-shaped lute;
a third rests, regarding the bank, the wood.

There is no lapis lazuli here, no gaiety.
No red-crowned crane in flight.
Only harmony and the interior trace

of fingerprints, fired in the clay,
undiminished, still of human size.

Awaiting Rain

You said she taught about rain,
how to tell it was going to fall
from the earth-scent
that hovers fresh before a storm
and the ways leaves turn
to wave the lighter
underside of their blade,
coaxing drops to descend
and then rise through root and vein
to meet thirst.

Before rain, she said, you will stop in mid-step
to wonder that you smell wild lilac and maypop
traveling on the breeze that blows
from Brinegar's field.
Pay attention to mating frogs
when they croak louder, she said,
to pinecones when they fold their scales inward.
These are signs of what is to come
as sure as the sky's lust at sunrise,
and the moon's ring of light
the night before.

I said, it seems she means we have no reason
to be surprised. We might prepare.
That's not it, you answered, insisting
the fragrance of the passionflower is sweet
and the red dawn, beautiful.
The halo in the night sky, worthy of praise.
It's not about the rain
but what is prior and the waiting.
Which I love, you said.

Olive Hill Flood, July 5, 1939

for Bessie Jacobs, in memoriam

Water means death.
I say it so what I say
I can abide.

Abide, abide with me.
Abide with me
fast falls the rain.

The darkness deepens
Lord with me. Confide,
the solid rocks where

I would stand—
they are no more.
The holdfast ground

runs like silt, the sand
in the whelming flow
of Tygarts Creek.

Railroad Street is a river,
ferrying away
what was here before.

It pours and pours, this sorrow
that pulls us down.
There are no bounds.

Impressions Revisited

for Alene Clayton Holderby, in memoriam

The prayer cloths, you said, were for
whispering thoughts at night
that, when I no longer see wisps of scarf
in the sky, I might remember the earthy
petrichor that scents air before hard rain,
air that heavies ahead of downpour
and the soddening of wizened bones
only to lighten again as clouds
enfolding the knob of Black Balsam;
that in darkness I might say with the hush,
lift me, like mist rising on the mountain's peak,
before I vanish and am gone.

Hedgerow

*I prefer winter and fall, when you feel the bone structure of the
landscape—the loneliness of it, the dead feeling of winter. Some
thing waits beneath it, the whole story doesn't show.*
—Andrew Wyeth

The walk ended at the hedgerow,
the tangle of bodark-heartwood and thorn
down-leaning where the pasture slopes.
The house out of sight, up and beyond,
inaccessible.

There we stood. You spoke of the scumbled sky,
how it reminded you of Wyeth's dry-brush,
scrubbing pigment into texture, muting
tones and moods—the loneliness
of winter.

I noticed the sparrow scrape and pictured
white-crowns raking snow for what
squirmed underneath. My boot-heel
kicked back—once, twice—gouging
the skeleton of the landscape

as if to leave a mark, convinced here
we could go no farther.

What Botticelli Did Not Portray

after Angela Strassheim's photograph, "Untitled (Alicia in the Pool)"

What if Venus had risen not from the froth of the sea
but from a pool on a farm in Iowa or Minnesota
with tower silos of grain as her backdrop as visible
from the kitchen window as in the camera lens
at the very moment wind sweeps her auburn hair
to stream like a banderole from her body's masthead
and her right knee bends inward protectively in counterpoise
to the slight tilt of her head and the jutting out
of the elbow as her hand takes rest on the slim hip,
a gesture that creates a triangle making the sheet
on the clothesline behind her a sail in our eyes,
if it is not already a piece of the expansive wings
branching from her shoulders—an angel's wings of white
like her suit—so that in this moment we wonder
only when and to where she might fly away
from the blue plastic pool whose water scarcely covers
her ankles and on whose surface innocently floats a silver ball,
to fly away, that is, away from her mother's laundry on the line,
the wicker basket, the bag of wooden clothes pins, and the twigs
and branches her father stacked in the corner of the yard,
the teeming storehouses of seed, kernel, and grist,
these the signs of custody left behind when rapture comes
or simply another day or the day after.

Venus Rising in the City

after Bonnie Blake's photograph of Liz Craft's sculpture,
"Mermaid," taken at the Whitney Museum of American Art,
June 2016

against the twilit sky you have risen
from no visible sea foam
an urban Venus welkin-ward
on the roof-top ledge
soft-boned you curl on your knees
feet splayed outward shoulders slanted
and torso leaning in so that your face
is large an oval of Mehron's clown white
cowl-framed with matted hair
continuous on one side as strands
of netting enmesh one shoulder
like a shawl before it is finally shrugged
and thus you may have escaped
I feel the seine that was to have held you fast

pink areolae emerge from the skin-surface
halter of chartreuse on black body wax
your face reaches forward as if to kiss
still coldly lips an em dash and mouth circled
with red greasepaint that extends
to cover both nostrils so that air
is filtered through the cherry sphere
this hole without aperture below
black bars that cross one open eye
like the iron grill of a cell's window
through which your vision will yet pass
to see the next horizon you are at once
contained and erumpent

to bring with you the barnacles of the sea
swirling shells in your hair between thumb

and forefinger in the crease
where your left thigh joins the hip
and as a lid over the right eye
pale phosphors dab your upper arm
like the glow of algae in night water
(how like human skin it seems
uncovered as a garment tatters
into the mottling of flesh and fabric)
and now Venus you are on fire
with the hint of flame crackling
round your right cheek and arm
a flash that is not of the sea
but the streets below a realm of forged-steel
verticals and horizontals and the sparks
of light that have lit you with desire

After Eden: Hopper's Pennsylvania Coal Town

After Eden

he made his way to Pennsylvania
tracing the coal seam with bruised feet
past the patch towns out from Pittsburgh—
Muse and Manifold, Colver, Collier and Hazelton,
a dam on Little Chartiers Creek.

He coughed the haze that hung over
heaps of spoil tip and gob pile
barren banks of bing and culm,
and in the shadow of a hopper car
he paused and peered ahead

into the late afternoon, just as years later
he would lean on his level-head rake
and stare down the corridor of yard
between houses, stunned at the bath
of light that now shone even here

on the fronds behind him and the tufts
of grass creeping over the concrete edge.
How warm the glow on his bare head,
how familiar and kind.

Gravestones

for Nelle Clayton Boyette, in memoriam

In a year of shuddering
I tell myself:

Study the rock from which you came
the stones that rise
from the ground

in the churchyard at Sharon
the double-arched marker of twin daughters
who survived 3 days and 6 days in 1852—

The first grave in this cemetery—

and to its right the remains of a child
who lived
one month in the spring of 1862.

Here lie the bones of the twins' father
who took his life in 1866—
Gone to rest, his monument says—

and of the mother who worked
without rest until 1909.
Give her of the fruit of her hands

her children chiseled in rock
to record her resolve, remembering
her left arm

was stump-ended from birth.
The fruit of her hand
it might have read.

When young, Aunt Nelle
would go to Eliza's corner
at the right of the fireplace

to watch her grandmother
sew petticoats with lace borders,
the cloth clasped by a *little bird*

that worked like a spring clothespin
fastened on the candle stand.
She pinned the other end to her dress

and brought *the little arm under*
like quilting. The little arm, *it was strong,*
she noted

in a letter to my mother
confessing *I could tell you more clearly*
than I can write it.

And now, over the chasm of years,
I reply
to tell myself:

these words
penned on paper
bring back the lost

or carved in rock
mark what was
and what is not.

They stitch
the vanishing trace
with golden thread.

Ashes

for David Kaylor, in memoriam

I always thought I'd be the first to go, you said
in the brume of Black Mountain.
Arms around each other's shoulders,
we huddled outside the church
and wondered when rain would fall,
as if to explain the plastic bag you held.

Ashes, you said.

I always thought I'd be the first to go, you said,
these words saying more in the silence
where the brush of years together earned hope:
I will not be alone (which means *you will not go*),
the absence unimaginable, until it is
(until it is weight you bear in hand)

Ashes, you said.

You said, *I always thought I'd be the first to go*,
yet here you stood, as on that day
you made an urn of spalted maple,
aware that such wood is beautiful
even in decay and might serve to hold
what remains

Ashes, you said.

Sentences

after Layli Long Soldier

This is a sentence: a sequence of words or a statement that is complete.

This, too, is a sentence: the pronouncement of a punishment that states the conditions under which one will live and be regarded for a period of time.

The first describes a unit of grammar; the second, an instance of its practice, as when an authority utters a sentence that judges another as guilty, lacking something necessary, or different from what is desired.

We associate the first with teachers, writers, and linguists, but the second with judges and officials of government who have power to use *sentence* as a verb.

When authorities use sentence as a verb, they employ it to say you are, for example, *a prisoner, an alien, someone unwelcome in our company, one of the shameful, one of the dead.*

You will live there and not here or *You will live in this way* fairly paraphrase what authorities mean when they use sentence as a verb.

Though these have subjects and verbs, such sentences are incomplete in ways that matter, saying at once too much and not enough.

A sentence may be technically complete, but not just or true or whole.

Juan Francisco Trevino, the governor of New Mexico in 1675, sentenced 47 Pueblo medicine men to be flogged, humiliated, imprisoned and sold into slavery for practicing sorcery; he sentenced some of these to death, hanging them in Jemez, Nambé Pueblo, and San Felipe.

The governor used *sentence* as a verb to make *sorcery* a form of *idolatry* and to make those who practiced it dead men.

The Pueblo medicine men had their own sentences to speak, such as *When Jesus came, the Corn Mothers went away.*

One of the punished, the Tewa Popé, led the Pueblo revolt of 1680 so that the Corn Mothers might return.

The preceding sentence also means that he drove out the Spanish, the friars, and their ways to please the Corn Mothers.

This lasted for a period of twelve years until *La Reconquista*.

With *La Reconquista*, Don Diego de Vargas, the new governor, renamed the mission's wooden madonna *La Conquistadora*, or *she who conquers*.

A panel of the bronze doors of the basilica in Santa Fe shows the rescue of the wooden madonna, a building on fire, and the date 1680, but does not refer to the Corn Mothers.

A tour guide at the Taos Pueblo says, "some say we have been here for a thousand years, but we believe we have been here since *time immemorial.*"

What *some say* and what she says are different kinds of sentences.

She means that the story of their being here goes back to the beginning, beyond remembered time.

This story speaks of the Mothers planting seeds in the underground and seeds growing and breaking through to light.

The Mothers followed the growth to emerge from *Shipapu*, the center of the world beneath the earth's surface.

Before the revolt, Popé sent out runners to the pueblos, each runner bearing knotted ropes.

The Pueblo were to untie one knot each day until there were no knots left.

At that point, they would know it was time to revolt.

Some sentences are spoken this way, without words.

A knotted rope is also a ladder.

In the pueblo, ladders lead down into the *kiva*, the chamber beneath the ground where one speaks as the subject of sentences not heard by others above.

The *kiva* is *Shipapu*, the place beneath, from which the Mothers emerged.

Ladders lead to *time immemorial*.

Like the Corn Mothers themselves, the other story surfaces from the kiva that is underground.

The other story makes ordinary sentences incomplete.

Those who use *sentence* as a verb cannot coexist with the kiva.

Their sentences are superficial.

It should not surprise that *kivas* were desecrated and destroyed during the *Conquista*, sentenced to perish.

It should not surprise that they did not perish.

The dead also go under the ground.

It is where we go, the living and the dead, to complete our sentences.

We go to the world that is *under* to find beginnings and ends, to hear the words the Mothers, the very old, and the fallen say for themselves.

These are not historical statements about Pueblo and *Conquistadores*, as much as warnings to ourselves:

That there is always another word spoken elsewhere

(That our sentences need this word)

That the earth cracks open, in portals to hidden sanctuaries, to reveal what is deep and beneath and beyond

What is emerging.

Medallion

You write a single word, *medallion*,
and add another, *brick*
or perhaps *stone*.
At Yew Dell we saw an outbuilding
with millstones embedded,
one in each of its four walls.
Someone denied windows,
you would have thought.
I wondered if you had in mind
this tight-made shed.

But then you write *dirt* and *medallion*
becomes a heaping of earth.
I see you on hands and knees,
wriggling bricks into place
to encircle the mound,
slowly settling river rock
inside the ring, hints of a cairn
to be feathered with flowers
and crested with cobalt,
a pedestal and basin,
that birds may find water
and enter your evocation
that rises from this ground,
open to air and aspiring to light.

Notes on the Poems

Tarblooder: The tarblooder was a worker involved in laying railroad track, securing the ties with smears of hot tar. Especially when working shirtless, he was vulnerable to searing splatters, burns, and the running of the scalding mixture down his body.

Precarity: Cerro Pedernal or simply Pedernal refers to a mesa in northern New Mexico in the Jemez Mountains. Georgia O'Keeffe would see it daily from the patio door of her home at Ghost Ranch near the village of Abiquiu. Piedra Lumbre or Shining Stone refers to the valley that includes Abiquiu.

Guardian of Our Breath: The figure of a doorman makes use of the Janus myth. Janus, commonly depicted as having two faces that looked in opposite directions, was the Roman god of thresholds and transitions.

Quiet Night: Paul the Hermit, one of the so-called desert fathers, was a 3rd and 4th century anchorite near Thebes. Li Bai was a major 8th century Chinese poet of the Tang Dynasty.

Night Fright and Night Prayer: These poems treat well-known episodes in the saga of the biblical patriarch, Jacob: his all-night wrestling match at the ford of the Jabbok (Gen. 32: 23-33) and his dream at Bethel of the ladder or ramp that connected heaven and earth (Gen. 28:10-22).

Easter Vigil: This is an acrostic poem on the Christian Easter proclamation, "Christ is risen, alleluia."

Our Sins to Be Confessed: The frame of this poem quotes from the Eucharistic prayer of confession in *The Book of Common Prayer*, Rite One.

At the Reading of the Gospel: A caracal is a wild cat native to Africa, Asia, and the Middle East. It is known for its long, tufted ears and its extraordinary leaping ability, up to ten feet in the air.

Thy Kingdom Come: This poem is an acrostic on a petition of the Lord's prayer: "Thy kingdom come; thy will be done" (Mt. 6:10).

Four Men, Three Made of Mud: *Penjing* is the Chinese art of creating miniature landscapes.

What Botticelli Did Not Portray and **Venus Rising in the City:** These two poems make use of two photographs that allude to Botticelli's famous painting, "The Birth of Venus."

Acknowledgments

I am grateful to the editors of the following journals who first published certain of these poems:

Barstow and Grand: "At the Reading of the Gospel"

basalt: "Awaiting Rain," "For the Time Being," and "Guardian of our Breath"

Beloit Poetry Journal: "Gravity"

The Ekphrastic Review: "Venus Rising in the City"

Jelly Bucket: "Quiet Night"

MacQueen's Quinterly: "Precarity" and "Sky Above Clouds"

New Madrid: "Witnessed in the First Month of the Year"

Pine Mountain Sand & Gravel: "Gravestones"

Presence: "Night Fight"

QU: "What Botticelli Did Not Portray"

Quiet Diamonds: "Doxology"

The Rappahannock Review: "After Eden: Hopper's Pennsylvania Coal Town"

River Heron Review: "Olive Hill Flood"

Saint Katherine Review: "Night Prayer," "Our Sins to be Confessed," and "Thy Kingdom Come"

Spiritus: "The Sound of One Poem Tapping"

Tahoma Literary Review: "Impressions Revisited"

Valiant Scribe: "And Also with You"

Willows Wept Review: "The Sound of a Tree Falling, As We Hear It"

Zone 3: "Hedgerow," "Neither Can the Floods Drown It" (here as "Ashes")

Several of these poems first appeared in the chapbook *A Field, Part Arable* (Lithic Press, 2017). Thank you to Danny Rosen, editor and publisher, for bringing them forth.

"Prayer Before a Sermon in the Nave," appeared originally in *Homage to Soren Kierkegaard: A Poetry Anthology*, eds. Dana Gioia and Mary Grace Margano (Wiseblood, 2023).

About the Author

Karl Plank is the author of the chapbooks *A Field, Part Arable* (Lithic Press, 2017) and *BOSS: Rewriting Rilke* (Red Bird Chapbooks, 2017). A past winner of the Thomas Carter Prize (*Shenandoah*), he is the J.W. Cannon Professor of Religious Studies, Emeritus, at Davidson College in Davidson, North Carolina.

www.ingramcontent.com/pod-product-compliance
Lightning Source LLC
Chambersburg PA
CBHW060352130626
46553CB00003B/1193

* 9 7 9 8 9 9 0 7 4 7 4 4 9 *